MIRROR, MIRROR

By David Neufeld
Illustrated by Pat DeWitt
and Robin DeWitt

Celebration Press
Pearson Learning Group

W9-CUI-984

CONTENTS

CHAPTER ONE
The Other Side

It was the carnival's last night in Shepherd, Kansas. Torn tickets lay in small heaps near the entrance gates to rides. "After tonight it's back to *Dullsville*," Diego said to his friend Hank. "I'm down to my last dollar. I can't even buy a pretzel."

"I can't either," Hank replied, holding up his own last dollar.

Diego said, "I mowed Mr. Dunstan's lawn three weeks for the money I just spent."

"But we had fun, didn't we?" Hank asked.

"Yeah," said Diego, "It's too bad the carnival shuts down tonight."

"I guess we should leave," Hank said. "I'm hungry, and Mr. Dunstan's market has snacks that cost under a dollar." Diego nodded his head, and they walked toward the exit gate.

The House of Mirrors attraction was in a faded 40-foot trailer near the exit gate. The attendant, a man with dyed green hair, sat on a stool in front of the ticket booth, humming a tune and playing a guitar. As Diego and Hank passed by, he looked up and said, "Hey kids, would you like to go through the House of Mirrors?"

Diego and Hank looked at each other and shrugged. "We can't," Hank told the man. "We don't have enough money."

"I'll let you in free," the attendant said. "Just watch the gate while I get something to eat. When I get back, you can go through."

"Well, if it's free—" Diego began hesitantly.

Hank cut him off. "It's a deal!" he said.

The boys leaned against the gate. "What did that guy do to get stuck with this booth?" Diego asked. They gazed across the carnival.

"I don't know," Hank said. "I guess it's better than the dunking booth."

"Yeah, but did you see his eyes?" Diego asked. "They looked—I don't know—empty."

"Maybe you'd look like that if you spent your summer at the ticket booth of an attraction nobody wanted to go into," Hank said. "When is that guy coming back? He's been gone a long time."

They looked for green hair in the crowd. Finally Hank said, "Come on. Let's go in."

"We're supposed to watch the gate," Diego replied.

"Why?" Hank said. "Everything's closing, and nobody wants to visit the House of Mirrors anyway."

A green light, the same color as the attendant's hair, glowed above the entrance. "Come on," Hank urged. "We'll be out before he gets back."

Hank walked through the doorway, and Diego followed. Country-western music drifted through the hallways. The first mirror made them look as skinny as pencils and about seven feet tall. Diego glanced toward the entrance—the attendant still hadn't returned. Then he walked deeper into the hall until he saw himself as a short, wide blob.

Hank ran past him. "Let's go to the end. They always put the really weird mirrors last."

"Wait up, Hank," Diego said. But Hank didn't slow down, and Diego found himself running, too. How could the trailer be so long?

"Diego!" Hank sounded scared.

Diego turned a corner and was face to face with a mirror—and a dead end. He turned around. He held his hands out in front of him so he wouldn't hit a mirror. He wasn't sure which direction led out.

"Hank!" Diego yelled. "HANK!"

Diego realized he was breathing hard. The mirrors fogged up. The red light on the ceiling made his face look as if it were on fire. It certainly felt that way.

"Diego," Hank called again, "you won't believe this. Keep coming!"

Diego turned around. He was looking at his own reflection. "Straight ahead," Hank's voice said.

Diego stuck his hand out. It touched the mirror. Then it felt as if he were pushing his hand through gelatin. His hand disappeared into the mirror. Then he felt someone grab his hand. He was yanked off his feet. He fell onto the floor in front of Hank.

They sat there and stared at each other.

They were in a bright, empty hallway. Odd music blared from a grillwork door at the end.

"This is weird. Let's go back," Diego said.

"I tried going back through the mirror, but it seems to be one-way," Hank said.

Diego ignored him and tried to push back through the wall. It was solid. "This must be a part of the maze," he said. He started to walk toward the grillwork door.

"Stop!" Hank said.

"Why? I want to know where we are," Diego said. He opened the door at the end of the hall and looked out. Hank peered over his shoulder.

Hank said, "This is like a weird dream."

"I don't think we're at the carnival anymore," Diego said quietly. "In fact, I don't know if we're even still in Kansas!"

CHAPTER TWO
Plancks

The place looked like the inside of a giant spaceship. Hank and Diego stood in what appeared to be the central hub and looked around them. Coming out from the center, like spokes of a wheel, were six long hallways, or arcades. Their walls were made of shiny stainless steel. They were so long that you'd need binoculars to see their ends.

People walked briskly around the building. They were wearing clothes that reminded Diego of his little brothers' one-piece pajamas. The floors were covered with thousands of tiny lights. When the people walked, colored patterns swirled out from their feet in all directions. Occasionally blue lights swept by from far down the hallways. When this happened, new groups of people appeared.

"We've been abducted by aliens!" Hank joked.

"I don't think so,"

Diego said. "These people look human."

"Maybe, but they sure have bad taste in clothes," Hank said.

Diego stopped a kid who looked about their age. "Excuse me, could you tell me where we are?"

The kid's eyes scanned their T-shirts and jeans, scuffed at the knees. He smiled, "Good copies. Where did you get them?"

"What?" Hank said.

The kid touched Hank's shirt. "Did you use nanosynthesis or microsampling?"

"Huh?" Hank said.

"Are they from Super Retro? Do they have any left?" The kid pointed down an arcade to a store. A model of a sports-utility vehicle hung over the entrance of Super Retro.

"What's the name of this place?" Hank asked.

The kid took his eyes from their clothes and said, "Kansian Centroplex 6," and then walked away.

Diego and Hank walked toward Super Retro. One wall of the store was covered with three-dimensional images of clothing they could find in their local shopping mall. "Can I help you?" a clerk asked. His hair was neon green, and he looked a little like the carnival attendant.

"Is that you?" Diego asked.

"No," the clerk said, "I'm X. X-689722, that is. U-0023566 will be on duty at 2300. Say! Where did you get those clothes?"

"Ready-mart," Hank said.

"Ready-mart!" the clerk said. "Look here."

"There's a Ready-mart here?" Diego asked.

The clerk pointed to a panel on the far wall. Three rows from the bottom, numbered 7865587, was a picture of a folding tray table. "This is what we have from Ready-mart. Would you like to add to your retro collection?"

"My mom's got half a dozen of those," Hank said.

"HALF A DOZEN! She must be a Money Controller," the clerk said.

Diego was looking at a wall of old movie posters—*Godzilla* and *The Wizard of Oz* and *Peter Pan*. He couldn't believe this was happening.

The green-haired clerk signaled to another who had just come in. The second clerk had purple hair

and clothes like the green clerk's. These weren't pajama-like. They were brownish and looked like they were made of videotape.

"This is U-0023566, another Double A, at your service," the green clerk said.

"Nice to meet *U*," Hank said. He bit his lip to keep from laughing.

"How do people pay for these things?" Diego asked, pointing to an old map on the wall. Maybe they could use it to get home.

The purple clerk nudged the green clerk. "Retro acting *all the way*," the purple clerk said and reached for Diego's right hand. Then he opened a tube that was making a low whirring sound and started to put Diego's finger into it.

"Whoa! Wait just a minute," Diego said. "Why can't I use something like this?" He pulled the wrinkled dollar bill from his jeans pocket.

The green clerk said, "Wow! I haven't seen one of those for 83 years!"

Hank stared at Diego's dollar. "What year is this?" he asked the green clerk.

"That little piece of paper there is worth . . . ," the green clerk stopped for a few seconds, "10^{18} Plancks."

"How much is that?" Diego asked.

The green clerk's eyes closed completely for a second. "Ten with eighteen zeros after it. That's a lot of Plancks. Would you like Centroplex credit? You can buy whatever you like, *anywhere*. Here." The green clerk took the dollar bill and handed it to the purple clerk, who placed it in a chromium envelope and deposited it in a slot in the wall. Then the green clerk handed Diego a badge with fine lines across it. "That should do it," he said.

"Can we get something to eat with this?" Hank asked.

"You can get *everything* to eat with it," the green clerk said. "Try any AZZIP in the Plex."

Diego and Hank turned to leave. "Double A's?" Hank whispered. "What does that mean?"

"It's either their battery size or they *are* aliens," Diego said.

Behind his hand the green clerk said, "They could have gotten 10^{20} Plancks for it at Past Tense, easily."

Diego glanced back at the clerks. They were smiling at him. "Happy New Year!" he called.

The clerks made a honking sound that didn't seem human. "You're a month late, but thanks," the green clerk said. "I hope 2890 treats you well."

CHAPTER THREE
Truth or Consequences

"2890!" Hank said. "That explains a lot."

"No, it doesn't!" Diego said. "It certainly doesn't explain how this happened or how we get back!"

Hank said, "Well, at least we're still on Earth—just in the future. Do you think the *Kansian* in *Kansian Centroplex* means that we're still in Kansas?"

Diego looked around. He had read in science-fiction books that people could travel in time without *going* anywhere. When most of these time travelers returned to their own time (*if* they did), it was usually at the same time that they had left. He also had read that messing around in the past or future was big trouble, or could be. Looking around at the future of Kansas, Diego felt worried.

Hank took his dollar bill from his pocket. Then he touched Diego's badge. "We are *very* rich. I don't mean just plain old rich. I mean *very, very, no limit on buying, 10 with 18 zeros*, rich. Even if a door appeared right now with a sign that said, 'This way back to 2002,' I wouldn't go."

"Yeah, but there's no door and I'm starving," Diego said.

The boys gazed into the AZZIP window. "At least this looks familiar," Hank said.

Diego stood in front of a screen, and a machine scanned his badge. "I just hope they don't nano . . . nano . . . "

"Nanosynthesize," Hank said.

"Nanosynthesize the pizza," Diego said. "Did you see the waiter's eyes? They didn't blink."

Hank said nothing; he was too busy eating his pizza.

"I think they're robots," Diego said quietly.

Hank asked, "Do you think the attendant at the carnival was one of them?"

Diego nodded. "I wonder how many kids have disappeared into his House of Mirrors?"

After eating, the boys wandered down another hallway. They stopped in front of a sign that read "Virtual Travel Bureau." A girl stood beside the entrance holding a screen in her hand. She was drawing something on it.

"Do you want to see where people in 2890 go on vacation?" Hank asked.

"I'm not traveling any farther away from home than I am right now," Diego said.

"Aw, come on!" Hank said. "We're rich. We can do whatever we like here!"

"Well, I'd cash my whole badge in for a ticket to 2002," Diego said.

The girl by the entrance overheard Diego. "They won't let you," she said.

Diego looked at her, puzzled. Then Hank dragged him through the entrance and into an auditorium where about a dozen people were seated. One person moved his legs as if he were running. Another reached out to grasp some object that wasn't there.

"Welcome to virtual reality, boys," a voice called. The boys looked around. "Up here," the voice said. The boys looked up. A young woman floated ten feet above them.

"Where to?" she said.

"2002?" Diego said hesitantly.

"Ah, the beginning," she said.

"Beginning of what?" Diego asked.

"Virtual reality, holograms, our digital records," she said. "Nice retro clothing."

"Yeah, well," Diego said, touching his shirt, "what about time travel?"

"Against the law, of course. It has been for 235 years. The Money Controllers outlawed it."

"Right," Hank said, "but what if someone from before 235 years ago traveled to now? How could they break a law that wasn't made yet?"

"They'd still be breaking our law," she said.

"What happens to them?" Diego asked.

"We find the time-door and seal it. Then we lock the travelers up!" she said.

"Of course," Diego said. He remembered another thing he had read about time travel— rules in the future don't have to be fair.

The woman said, "If you would like to see the consequences of time travel, just look into the display in that corner. It's free."

"Beware of things that are free," Diego said.

"It won't suck us in, will it?" Hank asked.

The woman shook her head. The boys went over to the display and looked in. They saw people crowded into a stuffy prison under the ocean. Diego groaned, "Wow, that is *bad*."

Hank grabbed Diego's sleeve and led him out of the travel bureau. The girl still stood there. She eyed them suspiciously.

When they were out of earshot, Hank said, "I think she may be a spy."

Diego looked over his shoulder. The girl was watching them.

"Maybe we should go back to the wall and check it," Hank said.

"Are you nuts? You're worried that the girl is watching us, but what about the cameras and microphones that might be all over the place? I'm not feeling very well." Diego peered into the corners of the hallway. "We can't go back there until we really know how to leave," he said.

"What are we going to do when this place closes? Where will we sleep?" Hank asked. He shuffled along beside Diego.

"I don't think it closes—ever," Diego said. The boys walked back past the central hub toward the Super Retro store. The purple clerk was on duty alone.

"Having a good time?" the purple clerk called.

Diego walked up to him and asked, "Do you know of a good place to get some sleep?"

"Why, yes," the purple clerk said. "Every wing of the Plex has a dozen somniterminals. Take your pick." The clerk smiled a mechanical smile. "*Definitely* robots," Diego thought.

CHAPTER FOUR
The Sleep Trade

The boys walked along a hallway labeled *Y* until they found a somniterminal.

"Why don't they just call them motels?" Hank wondered out loud.

"There's no door," Diego said. "How do we get in?" The boys stood in front of a somniterminal. It was just a wall with a row of eyepieces. The eyepieces had several buttons on each side.

Diego stepped up to an eyepiece. A voice said, "Badge scanned. Select amount of sleep desired."

Diego looked at Hank, "Eight hours is what I usually sleep." Diego pushed eight.

"Minutes, hours, days, or years. Select one," the voice said.

"Years!" Hank said. "Who would want years?"

"Since my twin brothers were born, my mom's been so busy she says she could sleep for years if somebody would let her," Diego said. He pressed the hours button.

"Place your face against the eyepiece, please," the voice said.

Diego leaned his face against the eyepiece. The scene inside was of a blue sky with wisps of clouds. The sky turned purple, then dark blue, then blue-black with millions of stars. His body felt light. For a few minutes there seemed to be a swirl of wind blowing around inside his head. It tingled. A dream began, and he was in a rowboat on a lake. Then the color changed to butter yellow, and the voice said, "Good morning."

"That was great!" Diego said as he stepped away from the somniterminal. "I feel terrific! I never thought I could sleep eight hours standing up."

"That wasn't eight hours. It was more like two minutes," Hank said. "Can I have a turn?"

"I almost had a dream, too. Do you think people here ever sleep in beds?" Diego asked.

"Why should they? Two minutes on this thing and they'd have the rest of the day free," Hank replied.

"What if they had to work the other 23 hours and 58 minutes?" Diego said.

"Or go to school! Or mow the lawns!" Hank went on.

Diego looked around. "I wouldn't worry too much about lawns." Hank scanned his badge and took his turn.

Diego spent the two minutes or so watching the people in the Plex go into and out of stores. "How come they all look so young?" he asked Hank. But Hank was asleep.

CHAPTER FIVE

Back in School

"Did you find a somniterminal all right?" the purple clerk asked. The boys nodded. "You're not from around here, are you?" the clerk said.

"We probably look like we just landed here from the moon," Hank said.

"My first guess was Europa," the clerk said. "I said to myself, 'these boys are the children of colonists.' Am I right?"

Hank looked at Diego. Diego nodded and said, "We missed a few things, being away all our lives. Would you teach us, fill us in?"

The purple clerk's eyes closed for a full second. He looked delighted. Being a teacher was obviously very retro. "Yes, I've seen digital clips of teachers." His eyes closed and opened again. "Good morning, class," His voice sounded different, more like Diego and Hank's teacher at Ruby Middle School. "My name is U-0023566, and I'll be your teacher for the next millennium. You can call me U."

Hank raised his hand.

"Yes?" the purple clerk said, "Your name is?"

"Hank."

"Yes, Hank?"

"What's a Double A?"

"Advanced Android, of course."

"You mean you're a robot?"

"A ROBOT? How would you like it if I called you a Neanderthal?"

Hank was silent. Diego raised his hand. "Do people here ever sleep in beds?"

"No. Why should they? Somniterminals were invented because one-fifth of the earth was being used for sleeping."

"How long do people live here?"

"That's a trick question, right?" the purple teacher said. "Human lives are shorter in years than they were in Old Time. Back then people spent one-third of their time sleeping. Now the somniterminal gives them eight hours of sleep in two minutes, and they get all that extra time for work and play. It's wonderful. Of course, people here don't usually live as long as they did in Old Time. Now 31 years is equal to 93 years in Old Time.

Diego thought to himself, "*Every day I stay here, I lose two days of my life.*" Then he asked, "When was time travel invented?"

"It was figured out by accident. A scientist left a pencil in a neutrino accelerator and thought it vaporized. But a day later it reappeared."

"Did it go back or forward in time?"

"Forward. If it went back, it wouldn't have reappeared."

"So how did they learn to go both ways?" Diego asked.

"Only advanced life forms, which include Double A's, can go both ways. But it is illegal. You know that."

The boys nodded. Diego thought about the display in the travel bureau. He remembered the time travelers in a special prison at the bottom of the ocean. A shiver ran up his spine.

"What would happen to you if you time traveled?" Diego said.

"I would be turned into a traffic light!" the clerk said. His eyes got very big.

"You're dismissed. There will be a quiz tomorrow on what we learned," the clerk said as the boys left.

"That was a short class," Hank said.

"Short! There's a college in Arcade Z where you can get a master's degree in 15 minutes!" the green clerk shouted after them. "It saves years of your life. Who's got the time anymore?"

The boys wandered down another arcade. Hank asked, "Do you think our parents are worried about us?"

"I thought about that," Diego said. "If we get back at the same time as we left, then it's like we were never gone. If not, we're in big trouble."

"Let's go visit Europa," Hank said. "After all, it's where we supposedly came from, right?"

Diego agreed since he didn't have any better ideas.

Diego and Hank chose virtual reality chairs next to each other. The travel woman lowered bowl-like instruments over their heads and brought visor screens down in front of their faces. She clamped arm and leg tubes around their limbs. "Europa, moon of Jupiter, it is," she said.

Diego found himself walking inside a crystal tunnel. Hank walked beside him. "Extra cool!" Hank said.

Diego felt unhappy and homesick. If the Plex felt like miles from home, this place felt like light years.

The tunnel led them to an underground lake. Nets brought up bright blue fish. A derrick stood in the middle of the water. Hank waved to a man who was getting out of a nearby electric boat. He wore a face mask attached to filters. Diego touched his face. He was wearing one, too.

"What kind of fish have you got there?" Hank called.

The man said, "Europa salmon."

"Do you live around here?" Hank asked.

The man pointed upward. A city hung from the ceiling above the lake.

"This way," the man pointed to a doorway nearby. The sign said "To Feros."

The man rode the elevator with them.

"It's not much to look at," Hank said.

Diego agreed. "It looks more like a warehouse than a city." The only buildings were stainless steel boxes stacked six high.

"Feros is home of Meteoric Mineral and Metals Mining Company. Workers process metals coming from the asteroid belt. The lake you saw fuels the life-support system here," the man explained.

"Do you miss Earth?" Diego asked.

The man shrugged. "Only the bright sunshine. What else is there to miss? The Plexes? They're not for miners or fishermen like me. What could I afford there?"

The man led them out onto an observation deck. "The communications center is over there." He pointed to a deck about 100 feet away. The boys were not looking at the deck, though. Jupiter, the huge planet, a thousand times bigger than earth, surrounded by liquid gases, filled half the viewing space of the windows.

"I don't come up here very often," the man said. "We don't get many tourists in Feros."

"What do you do during your time off?" Diego asked.

"Workers don't have time off. The Cubes," the man pointed to the stacked boxes in the lanes below, "are sleep terminals. Workers spend 3 minutes a day asleep and 23 hours and 57 minutes working. Workers sign contracts for 10 years. Then they retire. It's very efficient."

"Where will you go when you retire?" Diego asked.

"A lot of the guys talk about going somewhere warm and green, somewhere that has just a few buildings. We hear there are places like that," the man said.

"We come from a place like that," Diego said.

"Where would that be?" the man asked.

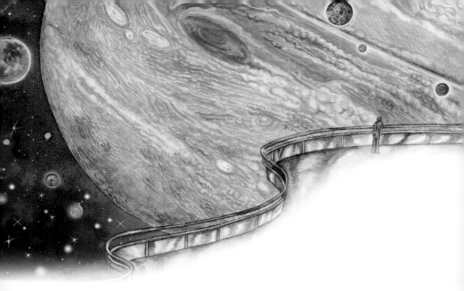

"Earth," Hank said.

"I could never afford one of *those* places on *Earth*. Only Money Controllers live *there*," the man said.

"How old are you?" Diego asked.

"Well, technically, I'm not really alive," the man said.

"What do you mean?" Hank asked.

"This is virtual reality, remember? I act and feel and think like a human, but I am only an image."

"What does that feel like?" Diego asked.

"To be honest, it's sort of lonely, especially here on Europa. Living in a virtual world really isn't much fun. You never quite feel at home—nothing feels quite right.

"I know what you mean," Diego answered.

Hank nodded thoughtfully.

"Pax," the man said. "That's what they call that retirement planet. It's out there somewhere, many light-years away. It has grass, trees, warm starshine, the works. Of course, I could only go to virtual Pax. I'd probably be unhappy there, too."

Hank looked at Diego and said, "Let's go."

The man walked the boys back to the elevator. At the bottom the boys turned toward the tunnel. "Thanks," Diego said. "May I ask you another question?"

"It's your Planck. Go ahead," the man replied.

"Could you ever become real?" Diego said.

"Sorry, kid. That's classified information," the man answered, and with that he disappeared. So did the tunnel and Europa. Diego and Hank found themselves in the Virtual Travel Bureau chairs. The helmets lifted. The boys stood on wobbly legs and rubbed their faces.

"Whew!" Hank said. "That was weird. I'm definitely ready to go home!"

CHAPTER SIX

The Key

"Did you know that the virtual guide on Europa isn't happy?" Hank asked the floating woman.

"Yes, he's been telling people about his problems. It really puts a damper on people's vacations." The woman pressed a button on the Europa display. A flashing sign came on that said "Out of Order."

As they left, the girl they had seen earlier still stood outside the travel bureau. She looked at the monitors in the Centroplex wall that showed places she might visit.

"You've been watching us," Hank said.

The girl didn't say anything.

"Are you going somewhere?" Hank asked.

"No," the girl said.

"Why?" Hank said.

"I can't afford it," she answered.

"How much does it cost?" Hank asked.

"You just went in. Don't you know what you paid?" When Hank tapped Diego's badge, she said, "Centroplex credit! You must be—"

"We're not Money Controllers!" Diego said. "We're stuck here and we just want to go home."

"But how did you get one of those?" She pointed at the badge.

Hank pulled his dollar bill from his pocket. "We had two of these," he said.

The girl touched the dollar bill. "Is this a—?"

"It's just a dollar bill. Where we come from, it's not worth much. You can't even get a slice of pizza for it," Diego said.

"But how did you get it?" she asked.

"I mow lawns," Diego said.

"What's that?" the girl asked.

Diego and Hank looked at each other. "Grass," Diego said. He looked around. Then he knelt down and took off one of his sneakers. Pieces of grass from Mr. Dunstan's lawn were always inside.

"You see these?" he said, holding up some grass clippings. "This is grass. Where we come from, people have it growing around their houses.

"Mr. Dunstan has a lawn that used to be a hayfield. It takes me hours to mow it. Back and forth I go on his lawnmower. If I didn't have headphones for my CD player, I'd go nuts.

"Then I dump the cuttings in the woods, or I put them near his vegetable garden."

Hank put his hand on Diego's shoulder. "You'd better stop talking, Diego."

The girl's mouth had dropped farther open the more Diego spoke. Then her eyes narrowed. "Where *do* you come from?"

"Before they could answer the purple clerk approached. "Boys, it's time for your lessons." He looked at the girl. "I see you met someone from around here. But we have a teaching arrangement. Please excuse us," he told the girl.

"We're coming," Hank called.

The boys walked over to Super Retro.

"In 26 more seconds I would have had to give you two a late slip," the teacher said. "OK. Quick quiz: How was time travel invented? Hank?"

"A scientist named Neutrino lost his pencil underneath the accelerator of his sports car. After he couldn't make the payments, the dealership took the car away, and he found the pencil. That was a day later, but to Mr. Neutrino it felt more like a year."

"Imaginative but *wrong*!" the purple teacher said. "You'll get nowhere if you try to confuse me. I've got more gigahertz than you'll ever have."

"Can *you* answer the question?" the Double A said, pointing at Diego.

"You're supposed to teach us," Diego said. "We need your help. Can't we just ask you questions?"

"Why are you spoiling my fun?" the purple teacher asked.

"We need to learn more," Diego answered.

The purple teacher said, "So I've been reduced to the function of a database. All right. Go ahead."

"What separates one year from another?" Diego asked.

"Your memory," the purple teacher said.

Diego wanted to ask more about time travel, but he remembered how angry the Double A had gotten last time. "I know that this is . . . ," Diego hesitated, "2890 and last year was 2889."

"No, no. Your memory actually created time," the teacher said.

"I don't understand," Diego complained.

"I know you don't, so I'll try to say it simply. My brain," the purple teacher tapped its chest, "remembers everything, *ev-er-ry-thing*, in the exact order that it happens. Every event is tagged by year, month, day, and time. I have been operational for 126 years, 4 months, 17 days, 5 hours, and 51 seconds. I can open my memory to any moment in all that time. It's only a file. Do you understand?"

The boys nodded. Computers really hadn't changed much in more than 800 years. They just had more speed, more memory, and an *attitude*.

The purple teacher walked toward them. "You humans have an odd filing system. You group events together according to the way they *feel*— sad file, happy file, scared file, shy file, embarrassing file. What a mixed-up system!

"You have no control. You can only hope to find the memories you need for a task when you need them."

Diego forgot what he had asked. "But what does that have to do with time travel?"

"TIME TRAVEL? HAVE I FAILED IN MY DUTIES AS A TEACHER?" the teacher bellowed.

The boys glanced toward the entrance to see if they were attracting a crowd. Maybe bellowing androids were common.

"Is it against the law to *explain* time travel?" Diego said.

"No," said the teacher, "but I must report anyone suspicious who asks about it."

"Are you going to report us?" Hank said.

"Not yet, but you're close."

"I've heard that Double A's have time traveled. It must be easy for you," Diego said.

"Of course," said the teacher. "If I knew where a time door was, my perfect memory would make it easy. It is also what I'd lose if I got caught."

"You're right!" Diego shouted. "We won't tell anyone that you know how to time travel."

"That's not what I . . ."

"Thanks! Thanks! We've got to go now," Diego said. "Don't worry about your memory chips. We won't tell our *Money Controller* parents about you." Diego grabbed Hank's shirt.

The purple teacher looked around nervously. "I'll erase my file of this lesson just in case I'm probed," he called as the boys ran toward the time travel hallway.

CHAPTER SEVEN
The Wall

"What are you doing?" Hank asked.

"He gave us the answer!" Diego whispered. "I think I know how to get back." A blue light swept up corridor Y. A few people arrived and wandered into stores.

The hub of Centroplex 6 was just ahead of them. The grillwork door hadn't moved, and the boys quickly approached it. Diego opened the door. Hank went in and Diego followed.

"What's the plan?" Hank said.

"If we recall our memory of home perfectly while we walk toward the wall where the mirror was, then we can get through," Diego explained.

"Can you do that?" Hank asked.

"I'll try," Diego said. He stood a few feet from the back wall of the hallway and closed his eyes. After a minute he started walking toward the wall. Whack!

"Diego, you never had a perfect memory," Hank said. "I don't think you're a match for the Double A's."

Diego stood there and rubbed his scratched nose. "Maybe we can remember how it *felt* to be on the other side—at home." He sat down with his back against the wall, and Hank sat beside him.

"What next?" Hank asked.

"Shhh." Diego closed his eyes and remembered his feelings just before he arrived in the future. He was scared. Maybe more scared than the time when his father was driving down a big hill in a snowstorm. The car started to slide sideways off the road. It hit the guardrail and slid along it, making sparks, until it stopped at the bottom of the hill. Diego had never been more scared than that until he'd gone into the House of Mirrors.

Diego tried to imagine his house and his little brothers. He was afraid he wouldn't see them ever again. After just two days in the Centroplex, Diego knew that life would be terrible here, even with his pile of Plancks.

"Diego," Hank said, "somebody's coming!"

They heard the door at the end of the hallway opening. Both imagined spending the rest of their lives in a prison at the bottom of the ocean.

"Why are you in here?" a voice said. It was the girl who had been outside the Virtual Travel Bureau.

"Uh, we were tired," Diego said.

"I don't think so," the girl said. "What is this place?"

"A broom closet?" Hank said.

"You two are strangers," the girl said.

"We live through here." Diego pointed at the wall behind him.

"What's behind there?" the girl said.

"2002," Diego said without thinking.

The girl sat down in front of them. "The year 2002? You're time travelers?"

"Quiet! Don't say that!" Hank said.

"But that's what you are?"

"It was an accident," Hank said.

"Take me with you!" the girl said.

"We can't," Diego said. "We don't even know how to get back ourselves."

"We don't have perfect memories," Hank said.

"I just don't know how to not be scared," Diego said. The three of them were silent. "What's your name?" Diego asked.

"Stella," the girl said.

"What do you like to do here?" Hank said.

"Draw maps," Stella said. She took a small screen from her pocket and pushed a button on it. The screen lit up, and she drew on it with a small wand. "I just draw what I imagine," Stella said. "I've always wanted to travel. Anywhere. I signed up for a colony in Andromeda, but my parents wouldn't let me go. They said that they couldn't afford to bring me back if I didn't like it. They also said that colonies never turn out to be the way they are advertised on Earth.

"I'm on a waiting list with three million other kids who want to train as interstellar couriers. If I were as rich as a Money Controller, I could go to a private courier school," Stella sighed.

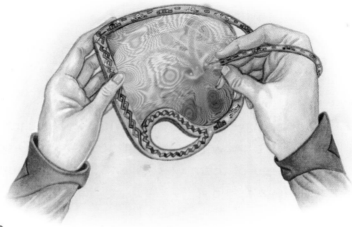

CHAPTER EIGHT
The Door Opens

"I don't like Money Controllers," Diego said. "I bet they time-traveled and fixed their future and then outlawed time travel."

Diego thought about all the old stuff on the walls at Super Retro. If he didn't get back home, they might as well hang him up there too, with all the old movie posters.

He took his credit badge off and set it down. "There's got to be a pile of Plancks left in that badge," Diego said to Stella. Hank then set his dollar bill next to the badge also. Diego continued, "And we know the dollar is worth at least 10^{18} Plancks. Don't take anything less. Will that be enough for courier school?"

Stella nodded. "Plenty," she said. "But—"

"I have an idea," Diego said. "Maybe to make our memories real, we have to share them. If we tell Stella about our lives on Earth, maybe the door will open. Stella, if this works, the Plancks are yours. If we don't get out, we'll share them with you if you help us get settled here. We haven't been outside of this Plex. I'm a little afraid of what the rest of the world looks like here."

Stella put her arms around the boys' shoulders and hugged them. "I'll never forget this," she said.

Diego closed his eyes and began to describe some of his favorite memories. He described his brothers toddling into his room and climbing on his bed.

Hank began sharing his memories, too. He described the time his father helped him fly his first remote-control plane.

Suddenly everything was quiet. The wall had opened. The boys saw a small red light bulb hanging from the ceiling. They were surrounded by their own reflections. Hank laughed with joy.

"I hear country-western music," Diego said. "Let's get out of this House of Mirrors, pardner."

As the boys stepped out of the trailer, the green-haired attendant was returning. A fat slice of pizza slumped over his hand.

"Hi, boys," he said through a mouthful of cheese. "Anybody come along while I was gone?" The boys shook their heads. "Do you want to go through? You earned it."

"Nope," Diego said. "I'm going home."

"Me, too," Hank said.

"Are you sure? It's better than you think. I don't know why people don't spend more time in there." He grinned.

"That's very funny," Diego said. "Did you ever wonder what it would be like to be a traffic light?"

"What do you mean?" the attendant asked.

"I *mean* that even double A—," Diego paused for a moment, "batteries get recycled."

The attendant's eyes widened for a full second and then closed. "You're out of your mind, kid," he said.

"Well, you're out of your time!" Hank said, winking at the attendant.

As Diego and Hank walked down the hill, Mr. Dunstan was sweeping the sidewalk in front of his store. Diego had never been so happy to see him.

"Hi, boys," Mr. Dunstan said. "Are you hungry?"

"Sure," Hank said, "but we'll grab something at home. We're all out of money."

"The sandwiches are on me, if you don't mind ones that were made this morning."

The boys ate their sandwiches. "Thanks, Mr. Dunstan. This is much better than that AZZIP pizza," Hank said.

"AZZIP?" Mr. Dunstan said, "Is there a new booth at the carnival?"

"Yeah, real new," Diego said.

"Well, it's closing time. Are you coming on Tuesday to mow, Diego?"

"I sure am. Thanks again, Mr. Dunstan. Goodnight."

"Do you think what we saw will happen?" Hank asked as they walked home.

"How can we stop it?" Diego said.

"Yeah. You're not supposed to mess with the future," Hank said.

"Hank, the rule is you're not supposed to mess with the past. That's what the Money Controllers did. People in the present are supposed to mess with the future. We do it all the time," said Diego.

"Right. I hope Stella gets to be a courier," Hank said.

"She will," Diego said.

The bullfrogs were in full chorus as Diego and Hank passed the pond on the edge of town. They reached Hank's house first. "Someday, I've got to tell somebody about this," Hank said.

"Well, be sure that it's another kid. Adults wouldn't believe you," Diego said.

"That's true, Diego. See you tomorrow," Hank said. "And by the way, I'm sorry I got us into that place."

"We're back now, anyway," Diego said. "My father sometimes tells me that I've just done something I can tell my grandchildren about. I know what he means now."

Diego's home was just down the road from Hank's. But on this night that distance seemed as big as the time between the present and the distant future. Once or twice he muttered to himself, "I'm not going to let anyone turn this town into a Centroplex."

When he reached his house, the lights were on in the living room. He could see his father lifting up one of his brothers.

Diego's mother met him at the door. "Carnival's over," she said. "Did you have a good time?"

Diego nodded. "Good time" wasn't quite how he would have put it. It was a time. And now he was back. Now he had all the time in the world. He hugged his mother a little longer than usual. Then he got down on the floor and played with his brothers before heading to bed for a good night's sleep.